GOD'S MY FRIEND!

DEDICATION

To Charles and Kenda as long ago promised.

Concordia Publishing House, St. Louis, Missouri
Concordia Publishing House Ltd., London, E. C. 1

Library of Congress Catalog Card No. 73-78025
ISBN 0-570-06992-0
MANUFACTURED IN THE UNITED STATES OF AMERICA

GOD'S MY FRIEND!

Written by Carol Greene
Art by Jack Glover

CONCORDIA
Publishing House
St. Louis London

CONTENTS

SOME WORDS FOR GROWNUPS

Five-year-old Malcolm and I had paused during our museum tour before a collection of religious sculptures.

"Why did they kill that man?" Malcolm asked, pointing to a Polish crucifix. I told him that the man was Jesus and reminded him of the stories he'd heard in Sunday school. He seemed satisfied and we walked a little further.

"Well, why did they kill *that* man?" he demanded, pointing to a Spanish crucifix of a later period.

It was a perfectly logical question. Two different artists of two different cultures had portrayed two very different images of Jesus. How was Malcolm with his literal 5-year-old's mind to make the transfer?

The basic purpose of *God's My Friend!* is to help the small child realize just that—God is his Friend. The book presents a number of Biblical truths gradually, to give the child time to grasp and build on them. But there is another purpose too, and that is to help the grown-up closest to the child (be this parent, grandparent, guardian, babysitter, teacher, or whoever) develop ways of talking with him about God and Jesus and what the Bible says.

Dialog with a small child about religious truths is not always easy and many grown-ups are frightened off. "Leave that to the Sunday school teacher," they say. But it is a fact that the best learning, the learning that goes deepest and stays longest, grows out of the child's home environment, whatever and with whomever that may be. So, if religious truths are to form an important part of the child's learning, they'd better have a place in his home environment. Malcolm's question just can't wait.

God's My Friend! uses a lot of ways and means to communicate its ideas: Bible stories, other stories that illustrate Bible concepts, poems, pictures, songs, prayers, discussion questions, and activities. All of these are, however, *only* ways and means to communicate God's love to the child. You may want to use all of those suggested for a particular devotion. Or you may want to eliminate some for reasons of your own. Maybe the landlord will evict you if you let Samantha make a drum.

Increasingly, though, you should feel the freedom to add or substitute your own ideas. Maybe an anecdote from your childhood fits the occasion. Or an experience the child has recently had. "Remember when you fell off your tricycle yesterday? Who came to help you? Weren't you glad that person came? God gives us people to help us because He loves us." The point is, when it comes to your child, you are the best authority. You know him, his interests, his experiences, his feelings. *God's My Friend!* can serve as a map, but you are the driver.

You'll soon discover that everything in the book is not designed for bedtime use, not unless you want paste on the pillows and scraps between the sheets. Some parts of the devotions will work fine at bedtime, but you'll want to schedule others at more appropriate times. This is all to the good, because the more different times in a day the child thinks and talks to you about his Friend God, the more he will realize that God *is* his Friend—all the time.

Maines, Sandell, Weaver, Kelly, McConnell, Bulau, Sakurai

WHO IS GOD?

God is the Creator of the whole world. He made the sun and the moon and all the twinkly stars. He made the big gray elephants and the little brown sparrows. He made the grass and the trees, and He made people. God made *everything.* He made YOU.

God is the King of the whole world. He is the King of the animals and the flowers and the people. He is the King of kings and queens and presidents. God is the King of *everything.* He is YOUR King.

God is the Father of the whole world. He is the Father of brown people and black people, pink people and yellow people. God is the Father of *everyone.* He is YOUR Father.

God is love. He loves the whole world. He loves the twinkly stars and the big gray elephants and the little brown sparrows. He loves all the people in the world—brown people and black people, pink people and yellow people. God loves *everyone.* He loves YOU!

Can you point to each of the pictures on these pages and say, "God loves *(whatever you are pointing at)*"? Last of all, point to YOU.

Prayer:

Dear God, thank You for making me and for being my King. Thank You for being my Father and for loving me. I love You too. Amen.

A STORY ABOUT

(Fill in your child's name and appropriate details.)

Once there were two people who wanted to have a little baby to love. So they prayed to God. "Please, God," they said, "send us a little baby to love."

God heard their prayer and one day a little boy (girl) was born. The mother and father decided to call their baby ______. "What a wonderful baby!" they said. "Thank You, God."

Soon ______ began to grow and *grow* and GROW. Sometimes he (she) did silly things. One day he (she) dumped a whole bowl of cereal over his (her) head. "What a silly baby!" sighed Mother as she cleaned up the mess. "But I love you anyway."

Sometimes ______ did nice things like kiss Mother and hug Father. Then Mother and Father would smile. "What a nice baby!" they'd say. "We love you very much."

Still ______ kept growing and *growing* and GROWING. Now he (she) is a big boy (girl), ___ years old. Sometimes he (she) does silly things. Sometimes he (she) does nice things. And Mother and Father still love him (her) very much.

But do you know who loves ______ most of all? God! He made ______ and sent him (her) to Mother and Father. He will always love ______.

Note to Grownups:

This would be a good time to show your child pictures of himself as a baby. Tell him about both silly and nice things he did. Explain that God loves him and helped him grow from picture to picture. Then give him a big hug and tell him how much you love him.

Prayer:

Thank You, God, for making me and sending me to my Mother and Father. And thank You for loving me. Amen.

SEE WHAT I HAVE!

(an action poem)

I have a nose, a remarkable nosey,
That sits in the midst of my face.
It wiggles and sniggles and sniffs at a posy
Without ever leaving its place.
(Wiggle nose and sniff.)

I have two eyes, two remarkable eyes,
That sit just above where my nose is.
They wink and they blink and they look at the skies
And the birds and the bugs and the roses.
(Wink and blink eyes and look around.)

I have two feet, two remarkable feet.
They go anyplace that I tell them.
And what's even better, they reach to the street.
If not, I would just have to sell them.
(Wiggle feet and touch them to floor.)

I have two hands, two remarkable hands,
Not four and not five and not seven.
I use them to play and to help and to pray
Each day to my Father in heaven.
(Hold up hands, then fold them.)

You have many wonderful things—hands and feet, nose and eyes. What other parts of your body can you point to and name? Do you know who gave you your wonderful body? God! He loves you so much that He gave you the very best body for you.

Prayer:

Thank You, God, for my wonderful body. Help me take good care of it. Amen.

GOD TAKES CARE OF DANIEL

Long ago in Bible times there lived a good man called Daniel. Daniel loved God very much and God loved Daniel. But there were some mean men in the kingdom who didn't love God and didn't love Daniel either.

"We'll fix Daniel," these men said to each other. "We'll tell the king bad things about him, and then the king will punish Daniel."

That's just what they did. The king was sad because he liked Daniel and didn't want to punish him. But he believed the mean men, and so he ordered his soldiers to throw Daniel into a pit full of hungry lions.

Now a pit full of hungry lions is an awful place to be, but Daniel wasn't afraid. "God will take care of me," he said. "And even if I die, I'll go to live in heaven with Him." And Daniel stayed in the pit all night.

Early the next morning the king came running to the pit.
"Daniel! Daniel! Are you all right?" he called. He was sure the lions had eaten him. Then he heard Daniel's voice.
"I'm fine!" said Daniel. "God sent an angel to me, and the angel closed all of the lions' mouths so they couldn't eat me."

"Help Daniel out of the pit!" ordered the king. "And send messengers to all corners of my kingdom. I want everyone to know how God took care of Daniel!"

God took good care of Daniel, didn't He? Who did God send to Daniel when he was in the pit of lions? What did the angel do?

God takes care of you too. He gives you people to help take care of you. Can you name some of these people? Who helps you get well when you're sick? Who tells you about God on Sunday? Who cooks your food every day? Who kisses you good night? All those people help God take care of you!

Prayer:

Dear God, please take care of me all day long and when I go to sleep too. Amen.

SILLYSCHMIDT

This is a picture of Sillyschmidt School. The children and even the teachers at Sillyschmidt School do all sorts of silly things. How many silly things can you count in this picture?

SCHOOL

Some silly things are funny, like the ones in this picture. We laugh at them. But some silly things can hurt people. They aren't funny at all. God doesn't like us to do silly things that hurt people. He wants everyone to be safe and happy. Can you think of any silly things that might hurt people?

Prayer:

Dear heavenly Father, please help me be careful not to do silly things that might hurt other people. Amen.

WHO IS JESUS?

A long time ago when the world was new, people lived together happily. They loved God and they never did anything bad.

But one day they forgot about loving God. They did bad things to each other, and they weren't happy anymore.

God still loved them though. He didn't want them to be unhappy.

"I have a plan," said God, "and someday I will make you happy again. I will send you a wonderful Present."

And one day, many years later, that's just what God did. He sent His very own Son Jesus to live on the earth.

Jesus came to earth as a little baby. He lived with Mary and Joseph until He grew up. Then He began to travel all over the country. He made sad people happy and sick people well. But most of all, He told everybody how much God loved them. That was part of God's plan.

Jesus loved everybody too, and He had many friends. But there were still a lot of bad people left, and they wanted to kill Jesus. So Jesus prayed to His Father.

"What shall I do, Father?" He asked. "These bad people want to kill Me. I will do whatever You say."

"Let the bad people kill You," said God. "That is part of My plan. And don't worry. Everything will be all right."

So Jesus did what His Father said, and one day the bad people killed Him. His friends were very sad.

But Jesus didn't stay dead! In just two days He came alive again, and were His friends happy then! They knew that God loved Jesus and that He loved them too.

Everybody forgets about God and does bad things sometimes. Can you think of something bad you've done? God is sad when you do bad things. He wants you to remember Him and love Him and do good things. So He sent Jesus to remind you how much He loves you. That was His plan. Because when you remember that God loves you so much, you just can't help loving God and loving Jesus and doing good things.

Prayer:

I'm sorry, God, for all the bad things I've done. Thank You for loving me anyway and for sending Jesus to remind me and everybody how much You love us. Amen.

DEBBIE AND THE SUGAR BOWL

One day Debbie decided to help her mother.

"What can I do?" she wondered. "I know! I'll fill the sugar bowl."

But Debbie made a mistake. She filled the bowl with salt instead of sugar. That night her father put two heaping spoonfuls in his coffee and took a big drink.

"PHEW!" he cried, and ran to get a drink of water. "Who put *salt* in the sugar bowl?" he asked when he got back.

Debbie looked worried. "I *thought* it was sugar," she said. "I wanted to help Mother. Are you angry?"

Her mother and father laughed. "No," said her father. "We're not angry, Debbie. But next time you decide to help Mother, ask her to help you do it!"

Did Debbie mean to put salt in the sugar bowl? Can you think of something you did wrong even though you didn't mean to? Can you think of something bad you did on purpose? *(If the child can't think of answers, help him remember.)*

God knows when you make mistakes and when you do bad things on purpose. He doesn't like you to do bad things on purpose. They make Him sad. But do you know what? God still loves you. He loves you even when you make mistakes and even when you do bad things on purpose. He sent His own Son, Jesus, to earth to show you and all people how much He loves you.

Prayer:

Thank You, God, for loving me all the time. Help me do good things always. Amen.

THE FOUR FRIENDS*

Once there were four animals—a donkey, a dog, a cat, and a rooster—who were good friends. They all worked hard for many years until they grew old and tired. Then one day their master said, "These animals are too old to work. I shall send them to the rags-and-bones factory."

"Oh, dear!" said the donkey. "That will never do. Friends, we must run away."

"You're right!" said the dog. "But where shall we go?"

"I know!" said the cat. "There is a town called Bremen not far away. We can go there and be musicians in the Bremen brass band."

* Adapted from *The Musicians of Bremen.*

“That’s a good idea,” said the others. “Let’s go!” So off they went.

They walked and walked till it began to get dark, and then they came to a cottage by the side of the road.

“Maybe we can spend the night here,” said the rooster. “I’ll look in the window and see if anyone is home.”

He flew up to the window, peeked in, then flew back to the others. He was very excited.

"The house is full of robbers!" he cried. "They're sitting at the table counting piles and piles of money!"

"We must chase them away!" said the donkey. "I have a plan. But we must all work together."

He whispered to the others. Quickly the dog crawled onto the donkey's back and the cat crawled onto the dog's back and the rooster flew onto the cat's back. Then POW! The donkey kicked open the cottage door.

"Agggggg!" cried the robbers, who thought a terrible monster had come to get them. WHOOSH! They jumped out the window. PLOP! They landed on the ground right in front of the sheriff and his men who had come to get them.

"All right, men!" said the sheriff. "Take these robbers to jail!" Then he turned to the four animals.

"Thank you for your help," he said. "You will get a reward."

Sure enough, a little later the president of the Bremen Bank came out to see the animals. And to thank them for their help, he gave them the cottage to live in and a big sack of money.

So the four friends lived happily together in the cottage and never did go to Bremen to be musicians.

Do you think the animals would have scared the robbers if they hadn't all worked together? Friends are wonderful. God wants us to have friends to love and to love us. Can you name some of your friends? What are some things you can do with your friends that you can't do by yourself? Do you know who God sent to be your very best Friend?

Prayer:

Thank You, God, for all of my friends. Bless them and take care of them, please. And thank You most of all for my very best Friend, Jesus. Amen.

THE SPIDER

A spider went a-walking,
He walked up a house.
A spider went a-walking,
He walked up a mouse.

Do you think that's a silly poem? Silly things can be funny—and fun. God wants us to have fun and be happy. Can you think of any silly things you do just for fun? But, of course, God doesn't want us to do anything that can hurt us or other people.

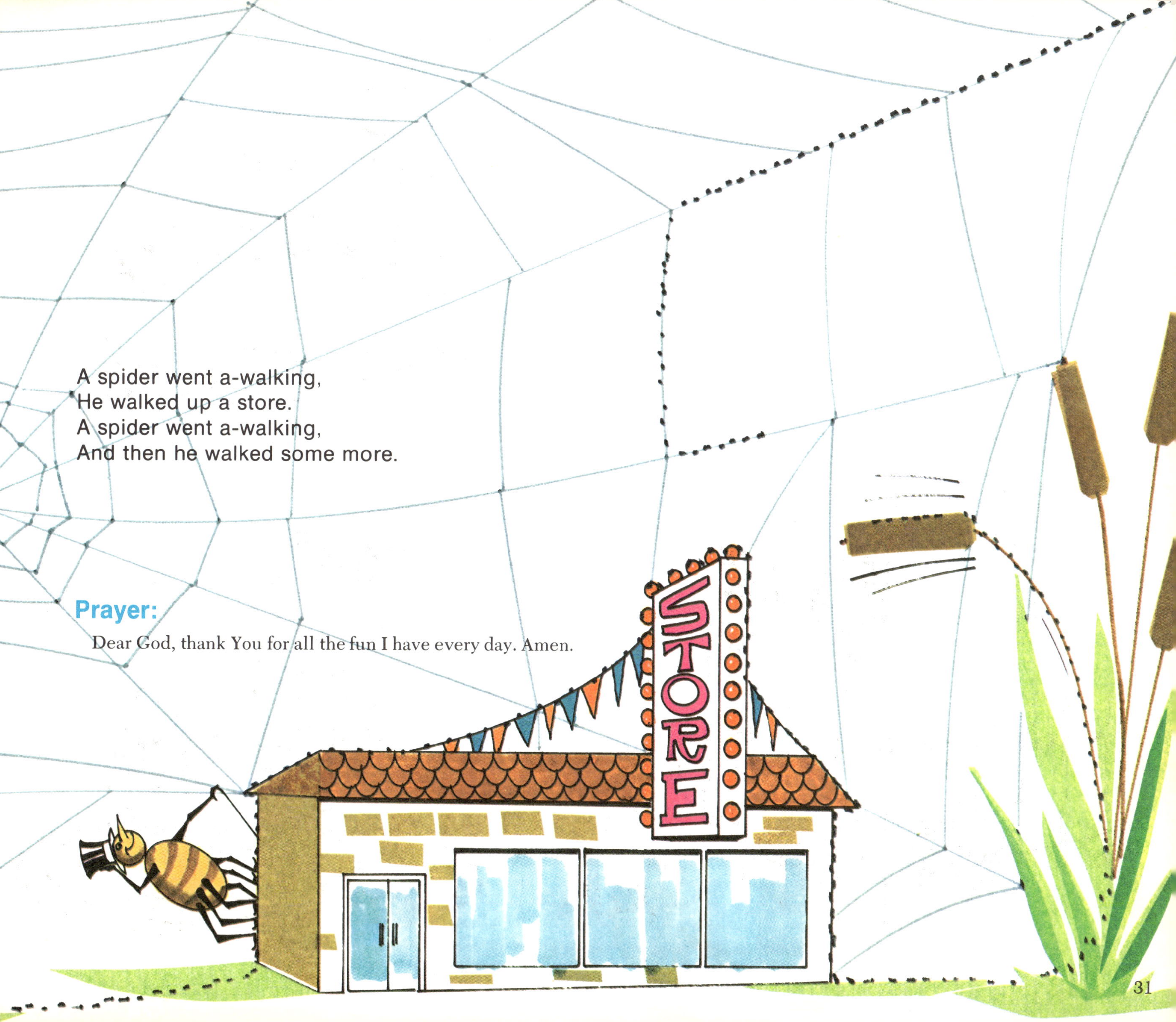

A spider went a-walking,
He walked up a store.
A spider went a-walking,
And then he walked some more.

Prayer:

Dear God, thank You for all the fun I have every day. Amen.

JESUS IS EVERYWHERE

Jesus stays by me, I know.
He watches as I play.
He's with me everyplace I go
Each minute of the day.

And yet He's other places too.
He's with the ships at sea,
With children visiting the zoo,
And grandmas drinking tea,

With little babies when they sleep,
And ministers at prayer,
And parachutists when they leap
Through miles and miles of air,

With all the people driving by
On Sunday afternoon,
With jet planes zooming through the sky,
And men up on the moon.

Yes, Jesus is with you and me.
He's here and over there.
Because He is God's Son, you see,
He can be everywhere!

Can you name all of the people on this page that Jesus is with? See the little box with nothing in it? That's for you to paste your picture in. Because Jesus is with you too—always!

Prayer:

Be near me, Lord Jesus.
I ask You to stay
Close by me forever
And love me, I pray.

Bless all the dear children
In Your tender care,
And take us to heaven
To live with You there.

(You can sing this prayer if you want.
The tune is "Away in a Manger.")

THE TINY ANGEL THAT TRIED

Once there was a tiny angel called Oswald. Oswald loved to sing, and more than anything he wanted to sing in the Angel Choir. So one day he went up to the Angel Choir Director and said, "Please, Mr. Angel Choir Director, may I sing in your choir?"

But the director shook his head. "No, Oswald, I'm afraid you can't. Your voice is so tiny that no one would hear you. And you're so tiny all over that one of the big angels might step on you and hurt you."

But Oswald didn't give up. As he walked away he said to himself, "I'll show that Angel Choir Director! Tomorrow I'll hide behind the big angels and sing with them anyway."

The next day that's just what Oswald did. At first everything was fine. He stood behind the big angels, and the director couldn't see him at all. And his voice was so tiny that the director couldn't hear him. But then a big angel stepped back and . . . tripped over Oswald!

"Ooops!" said the big angel in a very loud voice.

"What? Why it's *you,* Oswald!" said the director. "I *told* you you were too tiny to sing in my choir. Go away!"

"Wait!" cried the big angel with the loud voice. "Don't make Oswald go away. Maybe he *is* too tiny to sing. But he can play the bass drum. It makes a *big* noise. Oswald could sit on a high stool so no one would step on him."

Quick as quick he lifted Oswald onto the high stool and gave him the drumstick. Oswald hit the drum. THUMP! THUMP THUMP! All the angels began to sing. It was wonderful!

"*Thank* you, Oswald!" said the director when the song was over. "My angels sing *much* better when you play the drum. You are a good helper. Will you come every day and play for us?"

What do you think Oswald said?
Do you like to help people?
God likes His children to help each other. Helpers make Him very happy.
What do you do to help?

Would you like a drum to play? Here's how you can make one. First ask someone to help you. Then remove both ends of a coffee can and put plastic lids in their place. Secure them with masking tape. Tie some cord around the can and leave a big loop. Finished! You can wear your drum around your neck and hit it with your hand or a little stick. And you can play it when you sing songs to Jesus.

Prayer:

Dear Jesus, please help me to be a good helper to others. Amen.

WHAT'S "FORGIVE"?

Paul didn't *mean* for his dump truck to run into the table. BUMP. It just happened. CRASH. Oh, no! Mother's favorite vase! He'd broken Mother's favorite vase!

Paul ran over to Mother and started to cry. "Poor Mother!" he sobbed. "Poor vase! I'm sorry. I'm really, really sorry!"

Mother sat down and lifted Paul onto her lap. "It's all right, Paul," she said. "I forgive you."

Paul stopped crying. "What's 'forgive'?" he asked.

Mother thought for a minute. "Well," she said at last, "to forgive somebody is to not be mad at them for something bad they've done."

She thought some more. "Remember when your friend Terry popped your red balloon?"

"Yes!" said Paul. "I remember. But Terry's not my friend anymore. I'm mad at him because he popped my balloon."

Mother shook her head. "Then you don't forgive Terry," she said. "You wouldn't be mad at him if you'd forgiven him. I'm not mad at you for breaking my vase, because I forgive you."

Paul began to wiggle. "Can I forgive Terry now if I want to?" he asked.

"Of course," said Mother. "Just tell him you forgive him and stop being mad at him. You can go do it while I clean up the vase."

"Okay!" said Paul, and off he ran.

Can you think of anybody you'd like to forgive? Can you think of anybody you'd like to forgive you?

Because there are so many people and they all do bad things, God has a lot of forgiving to do. But He does it. Forgiving is part of His plan. Because Jesus died and came alive again, God forgives all the bad things people do. That's why He sent Jesus to us. Because He loves us and wants to forgive us. Of course, He likes for us to be sorry for the bad things we do, and He wants us to try not to do them again.

Can you think of anything bad you've done that you'd like to tell God you're sorry for? He'll forgive you. Because of Jesus He always does. Isn't that wonderful!

Prayer:

Dear God, I'm glad that because of Jesus You forgive me for the bad things I've done. I'm sorry that I did them. And I'll try hard not to do them again. Amen.

WHAT HAPPENED TO HELMUT?

Once there was a little lamb called Helmut. One fine day he said to himself:

Men who take care of sheep are called *shepherds*. The shepherd in this story was very worried about Helmut. He left all his other sheep to find him. Do you think the shepherd loved Helmut? Do you think Helmut loved the shepherd?

Jesus says that He is like a shepherd and we are like His sheep. When we do bad things it's like we get lost from Him. Then He comes to find us. "I love you," He says. "Please don't do bad things and get lost anymore."

Here is a prayer you can say every night before you go to bed to your good Shepherd, Jesus.

Prayer:

Jesus, tender Shepherd, hear me,
Bless Your little child tonight.
Through the darkness please be near me;
Keep me safe till morning's light.
Amen.

THE STAR THAT DIDN'T SHINE

All the stars were rushing about, having their baths and brushing their teeth. Night would soon be here, and each star wanted to shine as brightly as he could in the black velvet sky. One star was not rushing about though, and that was Joe. Joe sat in a little corner of the sky and pouted.

"Why should I bother to get all cleaned up?" Joe asked himself. "There are so many beautiful stars twinkling in the night sky that no one even notices me. No one will miss me if I don't shine tonight."

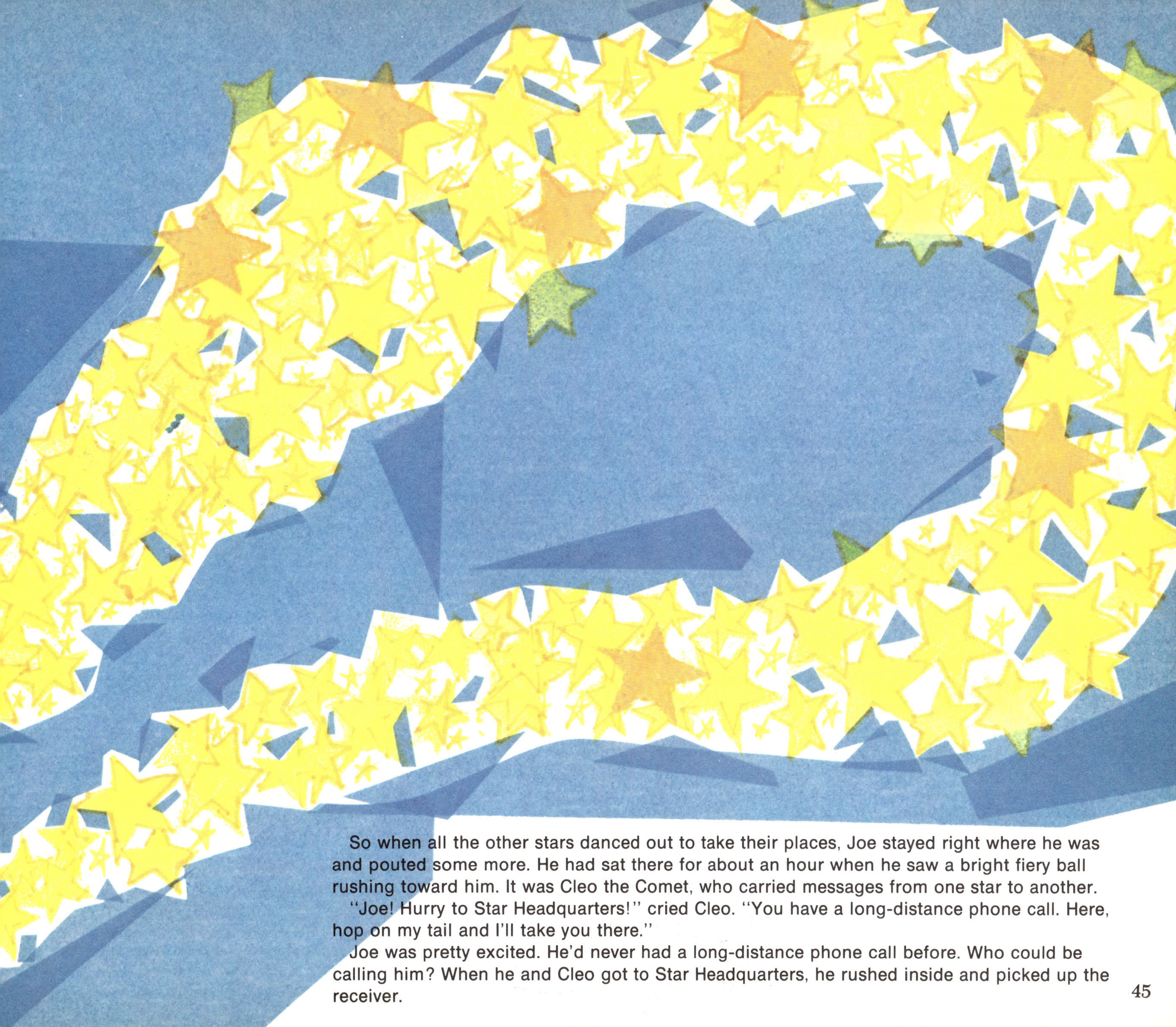

So when all the other stars danced out to take their places, Joe stayed right where he was and pouted some more. He had sat there for about an hour when he saw a bright fiery ball rushing toward him. It was Cleo the Comet, who carried messages from one star to another.

"Joe! Hurry to Star Headquarters!" cried Cleo. "You have a long-distance phone call. Here, hop on my tail and I'll take you there."

Joe was pretty excited. He'd never had a long-distance phone call before. Who could be calling him? When he and Cleo got to Star Headquarters, he rushed inside and picked up the receiver.

"Hello?" he said.

"Hello, Joe," said a faraway little girl's voice. "My name is Wendy, and I live on Earth. Where are you tonight, Joe? I miss you!"

"You miss me?" said Joe. "But there are so many stars in the night sky! How can you miss me?"

"But, Joe," said Wendy, "you are my special star. Every night after I get into bed and say my prayers, I look out the window to tell you good night. Then I go to sleep. But you weren't there tonight, and I can't go to sleep."

"Oh, dear!" cried Joe. "I didn't know I was so important to anybody! You hop into bed now, Wendy. I'll be right with you."

Off Joe dashed to have his bath and brush his teeth. In almost no time he screeched into his place in the night sky. Then he smiled down on Earth and twinkled a very special good-night to Wendy.

And he was quite certain he heard Wendy's voice floating up through all those miles to him: "Good night, Joe!"

Jesus said that His friends on earth are like lights to remind other people about Him. When other people see Jesus' friends doing good things and being happy, they say to themselves, "My goodness, that person certainly is happy, and he certainly does good things. And he is Jesus' friend. Maybe I should be Jesus' friend too!"

You're Jesus' friend. Wouldn't you like other people to be His friends too? How can you help them be His friends?

Here's another thing you can do. On a piece of paper draw a picture of Jesus and another person. Then ask a grownup to write on the other side of the paper: "Jesus loves you!" You can give the picture to someone you want to be Jesus' friend.

Prayer:

Jesus, please help me to shine brightly like a star so other people will see me and want to be Your friend too. Amen.

BACK TO

Here's Sillyschmidt School again! The children and teacher are still doing silly things. But this time some of the silly things could hurt people. Can you pick out all of the silly things and tell which ones could hurt people?

BILLYSCHMIDT SCHOOL

You wouldn't do silly things like that, would you? God doesn't want you to. He wants you and other people to be safe and happy.

Prayer:

Dear God, I don't want to do silly things that could hurt me or other people. Please help me not to. Amen.

TOBI

1. The Angels Come

Once there was a little shepherd called Tobi. He was too s to be a real shepherd, but since he had no mother or father, the big shepherds let him stay with them and help look after the lambs. Sometimes, though, they were too busy to bother with Tobi, and then he was lonely.

One evening just after supper he was looking for someone talk to.

"Go away, Tobi," said Tall Skinny Shepherd. "I'm busy counting the sheep."

"Go away, Tobi," said Middlesized Shepherd. "I'm busy playing my flute."

"Go away, Tobi," said Short Fat Shepherd. "I'm busy think about breakfast."

"All right," said Tobi. "I'll go to bed and I'll talk to Lamb a Dog. *They* like to talk to me."

"Animals don't talk, Tobi," said Tall Skinny Shepherd.

"They do too!" muttered Tobi. He wrapped a blanket around himself and lay down under a tree. Lamb and Dog curled up next to him.

"Of course we talk, Tobi," whispered Dog. "But only to you."

Tobi was too tired to talk for very long though, and soon he fell fast asleep. Much later he felt Lamb's nose poking him in the ribs.

"Wake up, Tobi!" she said. "Something wonderful has happened!"

Tobi opened one eye.

"The sky was full of angels!" said Dog. "Just a minute ago! They sang a beautiful song."

Tobi opened the other eye. Lamb began to prance around him.

"The angels said that God's Son has been born!" she cried. "He's come to earth to be everyone's Friend. All the shepherds are going to Bethlehem to see Him."

Tobi jumped up.

"Come on, Lamb! Come on, Dog!" he said. They ran after the big shepherds.

"Wait for us!" called Tobi. "We want to see God's Son too!"

"Okay, Tobi," said Short Fat Shepherd. "But hurry up! It's a long walk down to Bethlehem."

Tobi was excited because God's Son was born. That was the very first Christmas, and ever since then people get excited when they think about Christmas. Don't you?

But you don't have to go to Bethlehem to see Jesus. He's right here with you. You can talk to Him right now and tell Him whatever you want. What you did today. What you're going to do tomorrow. What you're going to do at Christmas. Go ahead!

Prayer:

Let the child express his own thoughts to Jesus.

TOBI

2. A Trip in the Dark

'he hills were dark and a cold wind blew as Tobi scrambled
er the big shepherds. Suddenly he stopped. Where was Dog?
en he heard barking off to the right. Oh, no! Dog was chasing
abbit! Tobi ran after him.

'Dog, come back!" he called. "This is no time to chase
bbits."

)og came panting up.

'I'm sorry," he said. "I didn't mean to, but it was such a
uncy rabbit."

They were hurrying along to catch up with the others when Tobi heard a frightened little voice.

"Help! Help!" it cried.

"It's Lamb!" said Tobi. "She's caught in a bush! We must help her."

Getting Lamb out of the bush was hard work, and by the time they'd finished, the other shepherds were far ahead. Tobi started to run.

"Wait for us!" he called. "Don't leave us behind!"

All of a sudden there was a big rock in front of him and . . . PLOP! Tobi fell right over it. Tears began to roll down his face.

"I've skinned my knee," he sobbed. "And the others are so far ahead I'll never catch up. I won't be able to go to Bethlehem and see God's Son at all!"

Lamb tried to brush his tears away, and Dog started to whine. But just then they heard footsteps, and up the path came three familiar figures.

"Well, well!" said Tall Skinny Shepherd. "It looks like we'll never get to Bethlehem if the big travelers don't help the little ones."

He picked Tobi up in his arms, and Middlesized Shepherd picked up Lamb, and Short Fat Shepherd picked up Dog. Then off they went.

Tobi snuggled up against Tall Skinny Shepherd and sighed happily. "I think we're going to make it to Bethlehem after all," he said.

It was good of the big shepherds to help Tobi and Lamb and Dog, don't you think? God sends big people to help you too. He sends them to help you learn about Jesus. They tell you stories about Jesus and show you pictures and help you sing songs and say prayers to Jesus. Can you name some of those big people?

Here's a Christmas song about Bethlehem and Jesus. Ask the big person who's reading to you to help you learn it.

O little town of Bethlehem,
How still we see you lie!
Above your deep and dreamless sleep
The silent stars go by;
Yet in your dark streets shining
The everlasting Light;
The hopes and fears of all the years
Are met in you tonight.

Note to Grownups:

Although the child will probably not understand all of the meaning and imagery in this carol, he will feel its atmosphere of Christmas hope and joy. You might explain to him that "the everlasting Light" means Jesus and that the last two lines mean that people had been waiting for Jesus to be born for a long time.

Prayer:

Thank You, God, for sending big people to help me. And thank You for sending Your Son, Jesus, to be everybody's Friend. Amen.

TOBI

3. Tobi Talks to Jesus

Nobody was in the Bethlehem streets when Tobi and his friends arrived.

"The angels said the Baby was in a manger," whispered Middlesized Shepherd. "So we must look for a stable."

Dog found it right away, a cave behind the Bethlehem inn. The shepherds hurried after him, but they stopped at the entrance of the cave.

"Oh, how beautiful!" said Tall Skinny Shepherd softly.

In the middle of the cave sat a lady, her eyes as dark as the night outside and her smile as gentle as the starlight. Behind her stood a tired-looking man and beside them, in a manger filled with straw, lay a little Baby. There were animals in the cave too—a cow and two donkeys and an ox.

"Hello, shepherds," said the tired-looking man. "I am Joseph, and this is my wife, Mary. You've come to see the Baby, haven't you? Please come into the cave."

Tobi held Dog by his collar and Lamb by her thick wool as he tiptoed into the cave.

"Wait!" whispered Short Fat Shepherd. "You mustn't bring those animals in by the Baby, Tobi."

"It's all right," said Mary. "My Son loves animals as much as this little boy does. He'll be happy to see them."

So Tobi walked right up to her.

"I'm Tobi," he said. "And this is Lamb and this is Dog. What is the Baby's name?"

"Jesus," answered Mary.

"He's an awfully nice Baby," said Tobi.

"Would you like to touch His hand?" asked Mary.

"Oh, yes!" whispered Tobi. Very carefully he put one finger on the Baby's tiny hand. And then a wonderful thing happened. Baby Jesus closed His little fingers around Tobi's big one, and He looked right into Tobi's eyes and smiled.

"Ahhhhh!" He said.

Tobi's eyes filled with tears. He had never been so happy!

Later outside the cave he pulled at Tall Skinny Shepherd's sleeve.

"Do you know what Jesus said to me?" he asked.

"What, Tobi?" said Tall Skinny Shepherd, smiling.

"He said, 'I love you, Tobi. I love you very much.' And I believe Him!"

"So do I, Tobi," said Tall Skinny Shepherd, and he lifted Tobi up in his arms.

Would you like to make a picture of the cave where Jesus was born? First trace the shapes on a blank piece of paper. Ask a grownup to help you. Then color them—Mary, Joseph, Baby Jesus, Tobi, Dog, and Lamb. Cut them out.

Next take a piece of brown paper and draw a cave with lots of straw on the floor. Paste your figures on the cave piece of paper wherever you want them to be.

You can hang your picture by your bed. Or on the refrigerator. Or give it to your favorite friend for Christmas.

Prayer:

I'm very happy that You came to earth on that first Christmas, Jesus. Thank You! Amen.

TOBI

4. The Old Lady

When Tobi and his friends left the little cave in Bethlehem, it was much too late to go back to their home in the hills. So Tall Skinny Shepherd suggested that they spend the rest of the night under a big tree just outside town.

"We can sleep a little while anyway," he said.

But no one could sleep at all. They were too excited and happy. After all, they'd just seen the Baby Jesus.

"Why don't we sing some happy songs?" said Middle-sized Shepherd, and he took out his flute. Everyone thought that was a good idea, and so they all sang—even Dog and Lamb.

Suddenly they heard a mean, mean voice say, "Stop making all that noise!"

There stood an old lady, wrapped up in a robe and looking very angry.

"You woke me up!" she said.

"We're sorry," said Tobi. "But we just saw the Baby Jesus, and we were so happy we *had* to sing."

"Who is the Baby Jesus?" asked the old lady.

"He's God's Son!" said Tobi. "Come on, I'll show you!" And he grabbed the old lady's hand and pulled her all the way back to the cave with him. He didn't go inside with her though, because he thought she might want to see Baby Jesus by herself.

In a few minutes she came back out, and she didn't look at all mean anymore. A big smile covered her whole face.

"What a wonderful Baby!" she said. "I'm so happy! Do you think I could sit under the tree and sing songs with you and your friends?"

"Of course!" said Tobi. And soon they were all sitting under the tree and singing the happiest songs you ever heard—the old lady and Tall Skinny Shepherd and Middlesized Shepherd and Short Fat Shepherd and Dog and Lamb and Tobi.

Don't you feel like singing too when you think about Christmas and the Baby Jesus? Why don't you? Here's one song you can sing. And you probably know others. Right?

LITTLE CHILDREN, CAN YOU TELL?

2. Yes, we know the story well;
Listen now, and hear us tell,
Ev'ry girl and ev'ry boy,
Why the shepherds sang for joy
On that Christmas morning.

3. For a little Babe that day
Cradled in a manger lay.
Born on earth our Lord to be;
This the wond'ring shepherds see
On that Christmas morning.

Prayer:

Dear Jesus, please help me to remember to tell other people how You came to earth at Christmas so they can be happy too. Amen.

God made pumpkins

God made pumpkins, God made grapes,
God made mice and hairy apes,
God made carrots, God made beets,
God made doves and parakeets.
THANK YOU, GOD!

God made goldfish, God made whales,
God made kangaroos and snails,
God made hippos, God made fleas,
God made butterflies and bees.
THANK YOU, GOD!

God made seas and God made sand,
God made rivers and dry land,
God made mothers, fathers too,
God made me and God made you.
THANK YOU, GOD!

God made *everything*. He did a good job too, don't you think? Here's a game you can play. Look around and pick out something. Then say: "I see something God made that's *blue*" (or red or green or pink with yellow polkadots or whatever color your something is). The other person has to guess what you see. He asks questions like: "Is it the sky?" or "Is it the rug?" When he gets the right answer, it's his turn to think of something. You can use anything you see in your game, because God even made the parts for the things people put together, like rugs.

Prayer:

Thank You, God, for the wonderful world You made. Amen.